ABOUT THE AUTHOR

Claire was born in Melbourne Australia, and now resides in Perth after also living in the UK for many years. She is a member of Mensa, works in finance and is an avid reader of science fiction and fantasy.

Claire has a dark and dry sense of humour, and spends her free time creating either poetry, short stories, or music with her band.

DEDICATION

This is for all of those I have loved and lost, those I love today, and the relationships yet to come…

Claire Turton

METTLE & FLESH

A Collection of Poetry

AUSTIN MACAULEY PUBLISHERS™
LONDON • CAMBRIDGE • NEW YORK • SHARJAH

Copyright © Claire Turton (2021)

The right of Claire Turton to be identified as author of this work has been asserted in accordance with section 77 and 78 of the Copyright, Designs and Patents Act 1988.

All rights reserved. No part of this publication may be reproduced, stored in a retrieval system, or transmitted in any form or by any means, electronic, mechanical, photocopying, recording, or otherwise, without the prior permission of the publishers.

Any person who commits any unauthorized act in relation to this publication may be liable to criminal prosecution and civil claims for damages.

A CIP catalogue record for this title is available from the British Library.

ISBN 9781398422339 (Paperback)
ISBN 9781398422346 (ePub e-book)

www.austinmacauley.com

First Published (2021)
Austin Macauley Publishers Ltd
25 Canada Square
Canary Wharf
London
E14 5LQ

ACKNOWLEDGEMENTS

To my beautiful family, whom always seem to triumph in spirit through adversary, and who bear each new burden with a smile.

PREFACE

To be honest, I feel most of these have written themselves, as I don't know where they came from.

Some I struggle to read aloud to others and are best heard in your own head. I hope the catharsis that I felt putting the words onto a page is echoed through the reader. If nothing else, I hope some make you smile.

I was called a chameleon once by my own family – anything anyone needs you to be. Writing helps to strip the need to pretend away and in a way is possibly the most honest form of communication I have found. I encourage everyone to do it.

POEMS

PART 1: CONTEMPLATION 13
- Every Woman 14
- Spied Her 16
- Inane 18
- Insanity 20
- Tell Me Bore 22
- Formless 23
- Salt 24
- The Rain 26
- Numbers 27
- In Memory Am 28

PART 2: LAMENTATION 29
- A Personal Haunting 30
- Hole Soul 31
- Trust 32
- That Which I Was 34
- Disappointment 36
- Farewell My Rock 38
- Dark Thoughts 40
- Truth and Lies 42
- Soul Thief 43
- Silence 46
- In My Skin 47

PART 3: RUMINATION 49
- Immortal Ruse 50
- Who Am I 52
- The Hue of You 54
- Our Own Worst 56
- Babysitter 57
- Mettle and Flesh 60
- Thoughts & Prayers 62
- Asleep 64
- Writer's Compulsion 65

PART 1
Contemplation

Every Woman

Oh, how I loved myself
A thing of youth and beauty
All slender grace and health
No work or family duty

Oh, how I lost the time
A thing of constant movement
With ever present chime
My face with no improvement

Oh, how the lines creep in
They say it means you live
I feel yet to begin
Yet now less years to give

Oh, how you see me less
Apparent worth has faded
No longer age you guess
It's hard not to feel jaded

Oh, how I am moved on
Society discarded
Young models lavished on
No jobs no love nor lauded

Oh, how am I to feel
Left out here in the cold
The pain from which I reel
At 40 I am old.

Spied Her

How delicate the dance you deal
Spinning your fine web, not steel
But silk and soft and yet so strong
I wonder you keep at it so long
And yet you never cease or tire
Your feet so agile and never mire
Themselves in fatigue, never stuck
Or covered in the endless muck
Or dirt or husks of your victims
The poor souls caught in perfect systems
Of woven death so deftly dealt
To watch it I have only felt
A sense of pity for the caught
And yet for me a sense of naught
But admiration for your weaving
The type of which should leave me seething
At the damage clearly done
With no regard for anyone
As you hide in plain sight in rooms
Or underneath flowers and blooms
Ever poised to expose your fangs
As stuck in gossamer threads he hangs
Helpless against the force of nature
Even one so small in stature
And so, you wrap and hold him near
Draining that I hold so dear
Of anything that made him mine
He's a display in your design
To join the others, you collected

The many men you had defected
And though I know you'll drain him dry
I can't be angry, will not cry
For watching you rebuild again
Repair the web and lure more men
I see a thing of beauty dark
More a raven then a lark
You cannot scavenge that which not dead
As such the pain is heart not head
So, spin again your invisible loom
Delicious deliverer of doom.

Inane

How inane I find your banter
A charmless foul enchanter
You may have pretty curls
Your witlessness unfurls

Enjoy it whilst you can
The love of every man
For once your looks fade
You will be in the shade

With nothing left to offer
No money in your coffer
Then you will lament
The rest of us resent

No longer you we carry
Your only plan to marry
Weighing our sex down
Now a wrinkly clown

Frozen features fall
You used to have it all
Seeing you a chore
Now nothing but a bore

And so I watch with glee
Your marks turn and flee
Left for a younger model
No one wants to coddle

A hollow empty shell
We all know it so well
And so I pity not
The girls that time forgot.

Insanity

Is insanity a condition
Or just a state of mind
Something that you catch
Something we can find
Can I make my way towards it
With enough time
Will I remember the journey
Will it send me blind
It is but interpretation
Of another's word
Could it be the ramblings of
Someone deemed absurd
How can someone know my thoughts
To tell that I'm insane
Ask their respected cohorts
Judge me on my brain
What if it is all a lie
To get us thinking straight
What if there is nothing that
Can change our sorry fate
For how can anyone declare
That they indeed know best
What my brain should think like
Whilst working or at rest
What if interpretation does
In of itself construe
A misinterpretation of
The thoughts that make you, you
We see and feel in different ways

Why not thoughts the same
Perhaps expression of these thoughts
Differ brain to brain
And so, I have but one conclusion
It's pretty clear to me
With sanity but mass delusion
There's no insanity

Tell Me Bore

Tell me more about yourself
Let's not waste time on truth
Tell me that you were so different
A misbegotten youth
Recount tales of funny times
Of witty conversations
Recall more of your prowess
Of 'countless' fornications
My aren't you the travelled one
A man of such endeavour
A girl can only hope to be
With one who is so clever
So tarry more on tales of old
That tell of your attraction
Of how you were so very bold
And saw all of the actions
So tell me more and once again
These tales you wish were true
And hope to god my desperate friend
I won't be bored with you.

Formless

Now everyone, desperate, experiments with form
To prove to other writers they have literary wit
No one wants to tell them in their bid not to conform
Most resulting masterpieces, literally shit

Ho! What creativity falls upon the page
New and bold and never seen the like of which before
Let's decry the tried and tested forms of yonder age
And most the population, alienate and bore

Heaven forbid one should harken back to talent
Twist words into clever weighted couplets rhymes and
  lines
No need to be perfect but to make language relent
Weave words to ideas like fluid moving vines

What of those who straighten pens and always fiercely
  clean
Where stray hairs are deftly tied, neat safe and away
Those of whom will never seem to understand or glean
Pleasure from prose clearly let alone to stray

Keep your esoteric wanderings of rambling word
Give me structure, more robust to please my mind
To me lack of form and rhyme will always seem absurd
I wonder, what, then in my poetry you find?

Salt

The salt seems to have a tang
tangibility
in the air
That instantly awakens all the senses,
in my hair
It gathers,
crusty,
forming knots as the wind
Tosses and twirls it around my head,
a crazy spin
Of movement to mimic this choppy sea,
churning
With a rage I also feel deep within
and it stirs
up old wounds where salt shouldn't still sting
And yet
the shifting sand between my toes
leeches much of the sting away
as course
and fine sensation rub
away so much tension
Drowning
out the inner voices
ever constant noise now white
with wave crashing
Hesitation
as it cleanses filthy shore
from footprints
past habitation

then draws back
into itself
rejoining body becoming one

The Rain

A myriad of colours fill the little twinkling tears
As they rain down mercilessly from devastated sky
Covering all they find in their downward path
Hurtling towards their doom, born are they to die

Gathering together they huddle into pools
Whispering their secrets of places they have swept
Moving parts of ground as they scurry out and through
Collections of enough invaders and the streets have wept

Sanitising all in their battle with the land
Cleaning all the evidence that you were ever there
Giving you an inkling of life after you're gone
Continuing without you, not giving any care

Bringing forth a deafening to close you to the world
A sound so resonating that it oft evokes sleep
Wrap you in cocoon of white noise and ozone smell
You could be anywhere, sense natures open weep

Numbers

The thing about numbers
Numbers, they don't judge
May come back to haunt you
But they don't hold a grudge
They tend not to ask questions
Answers are laid bare
They never flinch or wince
At accountant's glassy stare
They represent the living
Or legions of the dead
They represent the heart
They represent the head
They can be unforgiving
Can be manipulated
Into the hands of willing
Lies are stipulated
They could be overblown
Or underrepresented
A mighty leader voted in
A despot re elected
Sometimes, they are your friend
But then they can be foe
Until you reach the end
You never really know
You add them altogether
And so I have found true
They can be quite surprising
One plus one is rarely two

In Memory Am

In memory am I stuck
In memory do I hide
In memory I revel in times that make me smile inside
In memory I can see
The memory of a me
The memory of a soul within where joy it did reside
In memory do I feel
The memory it can steal
A memory where pain is dull and nothing now can heal
In memory am I lost
The memory has a cost
A memory recalled is warped its edges turned to frost
The memory it can lie
A memory it can die
A memory can leave a void to drain you 'til you're dry
In memory don't you trust
Your memory love or lust
Our memory kept alive by one the other turned to dust
Their memory is it quaint
Their memory bears no taint
Their memory a better picture of us does it paint
In memory are we real
Lest memory truth repeal
A memory of inner beauty that life did not reveal
In memory that I am
A memory that I am
A memory of a memory, In memoriam.

PART 2
Lamentation

A Personal Haunting

Motes eddy through shafts of light
Spinning, swirling, pure delight
Cascading wildly in golden glow
Dulling, ebbing, ever slow
Daylight coldly leaching away
I clasp my legs, hold tight, pray
For only in the evening gloom
The fear of feeling you does loom
Temperature drops and hairs do raise
I lose my sense of calm malaise
Closing eyes yields no relief
It heightens senses, sharpens grief
Once cosy room an empty shell
Is that your scent that I now smell?
I feel a presence start to linger
Pressure on my skin, a finger?
Not a finger but a hand
'Leave me alone' I can't demand
For fear this time you really go
That loss again, I cannot know
So sleep denied, one night more
Heart pounding, I will endure
Senses keen to touch, smell
Revelling in my own sweet hell
For here within, we are together
This fatal bond I cannot sever
No one understands but me
I love you still, sweet lunacy

Hole Soul

I came to the conclusion just a little while ago
That something wasn't right, but what I didn't know
It's hard to put my finger on and yet I feel it true
For every part of me points to it not being you
And so I roll it round and round, toss it through my head
Try to fully understand why part of me is dead
Now don't get too hung up on words, dead is just a phrase
But look into my eyes and see no soul, just a gaze
I know what should be said and done, I know you feel it too
But saying words and doing things doesn't make me true
I feel like quite the imposter, weaving through a life
Waiting for the moment that you see I'm not a wife
Not a lover or a friend, no companion here
Not malicious, not a threat, just not what you hold dear
Then I see it from afar, this ruse we have created
Not a love that went awry, spurned or abated
But an accident of chance, one you clung to, close
And I unwilling to explain, never too verbose
So lament not your choice of love, for how were you to see
The empty hollow deep inside the outer shell of me
I wait in hope that endless flow affection thrown my way
Can fill the void and make me whole, our souls will meet that day.

Trust

A strange old thing, known but unseen
Once lost is seldom found
There is no middling inbetween
Nor does it have a sound

A gift we give without a care
Yet often with remorse
Freely traded but beware
Of the receiving source

Perhaps you give the gift at work
Someone that you admire
Some person that in fact did shirk
Their duty on your hire

Your family up and down the tree
Expect it every day
They tread on it as plain to see
It's hard to take away

Perhaps they stole this gift from you
Through lies and some betrayal
They know not now what you will do
When their subversions fail

Perhaps it is yet justified
And doubt has never crept
For never to you have they lied
Nor cause you to have wept

Don't be marred by cynicism
But warn you now I must
Be careful of the gift you've given
That gift, my friend, of trust

That Which I Was

I am not that which I was before
You have changed me irreparably
I am less and yet so much more
New

You are not the person that I adore
That person was in my head
I don't even want you anymore
True

For quite a time I forgot how to feel
No pain no love no hope
New part of me this it did reveal
Cope

Eyes afresh I now see the world
Not better, not worse, but raw
Watch daily as my heart unfurls
More

A glimpse of you I catch in a street
Someone that I used to know
A former flame now bereft of heat
Go

What I am now is something to behold
Familiar yet strong and strange
No longer to reap, weep, but be bold
Sow

Disappointment

More than love or fear or hate
Disappointment bears a weight
Surprisingly not black or blue
Disappointment has a hue

One quite shady almost grey
That which is the dawn of day
Perhaps it's closer to the hue
That time of day that I lost you

Nearing close to 5 o'clock
The time that day and night do mock
Fittingly an inbetween
Where either or can be unseen

The time when shadows come to play
Creatures do come out to prey
Fitting then that sorry hue
I now attribute oh, to you

And so I carry on my back
Invisible to most, a knack
I learnt to hide the burden raw
That you don't need me anymore

This weight to add to all the rest
But this perhaps reminder best
That naught is ever what it seems
I'll see you now in my worst dreams

Farewell My Rock

Sedimentary
It's the only way to describe us
Sedentary
But the layers of time combine us

Stronger
But soft and ever eroding away
Longer
Than most but perhaps not another day

Porous
As events wash over and through
Timeless
And yet no more time with you

Metamorphic
Hardened we were with the pressure
Endorphic
But we now glean no more pleasure

Igneous
Fires burnt bright and then cooled
Devious
My but you certainly had me fooled

Everlasting
The promises we gave each other were
Devastating
The realisation this will not occur

Sands
The remnants of structures past
Hands
On our clock that have frozen at last

Soil
As all things return to the dirt
Toil
Over it, grow anew from the hurt.

Dark Thoughts

Here in the dark
in the dark it's calm
here I lie
I look at my palm
at my palm where the lines
they lie in wait
they lie and hope
someone will read my fate
and tell me the line
that represents life
that line which is broken
should signify strife
is more of a guide
a hope or a dream
rather than an end
written into a seam
irrational this
thought patterns are
when you lie in the dark
and look out afar
into inky night
which shifts and bends
it's not like the light
sanity rends
time slows to a crawl
the air seems to thicken
I think time does stall
I am terror stricken
I catch my breath

realisation dawns
I'm not alone
the dark has horns

Truth and Lies

Rue the day you wake alone
And know deep in your soul
You're the only one to blame
For digging your own hole

For whilst you hide behind the cry
I didn't see it coming
Your best friend could rightly decry
You spent the last year numbing

It's there to see as plain as day
The way he spoke and acted
You cannot now come out and say
Your love of him redacted

That naught was wrong and blind you were
When all the time you knew
When not with you he was with her
And nothing he said true

So lie awake and know inside
Your head and your soul through
That whilst you tried your best to hide
The liar here was you

Soul Thief

And should I die before I wake
I'm afraid my soul's not God's to take
I had it stolen long ago
By someone that I used to know

Wrapped up tight I held him close
Always wanting one more dose
Gaze into those blue green eyes
Every word welcome surprise

Gaze across the bed at you
Laugh at something you would do
Catch you home, moulding clay
Bunking work another day

Snuck in as you held a bird
Chuckled at just how absurd
Any minute here could be
What a crazy pair were we

And your temper flared so bright
Gave me such a nasty fright
Shout and bustle, I sit stone
Please don't leave me here alone

Then for months, you were gone
I was left here all alone
Other suitors were rejected
Never had my love defected

Twisted though did your heart get
Underwater did you fret
Who has access said you then
Worried about foe or friend

Melancholy was the night
Nothing gave me much delight
I waited ever patiently
Never wished that I were free

One New Year I spent alone
Given that you were not home
Never once a question why
To live without you was to die

And so the day your words came true
You said to me I don't love you
You drove me far far away
I begged for you to let me stay

And so I left you all alone
I left what was our happy home
I gave you back more than I took
I took one last lingering look

I felt for sure we would return
For both of us we did so yearn
Our hearts entwined it hurt to sever
I knew we would get back together

For it was written in our fate
We were each other's destined mate
And so communication starts
I felt the pull of our two hearts

Before the reaper intervened
And took my soul the clever fiend
For nothing could have pained me more
Than stealing that which I adore

Life no longer had a taste
Time grew slow for why the haste
Nothing more to move toward
Only memories now to hoard

Never forget the guttural keen
Something I had never seen
Come out of my hollow shell
You've left me here in my own hell

And on now with the march of time
Every tick and tock and chime
Brings me ever closer, near
When I drift your voice, I hear

I close my eyes and see your smile
It will only be a little while
So guide me then and guide me true
My soul of course belongs to you

Silence

Silence is not golden
It's sharp, loud and bright
When you are beholden
It's most painful at night

Silence is a gaping void
That drains you till you're dry
Emotion soon becomes devoid
Nothing left to cry

Silence is a throbbing beacon
Luring thoughts dark and low
Silences always topples reason
Fears begin to freely flow

Silence gives no consolation
It deafens with its weight
Leading you to desolation
Mere inches from hate

Silence is a state of being
Be wary one so still
Inside is a person screaming
Trapped against their will

In My Skin

Yet again I rake my claws across my naked skin
To satiate the burning pain that sears me from within
The body's largest organ as it covers head to toe
Wages constant battles against me as if a foe
Throwing up defences in the form of hardened welts
Resembles skins that hunters used to tan into their pelts
Cracking after sleepless nights until it's glowing red
Causing nauseation and an ever present dread
Drag myself again to work when feeling oh so ill
Learning to get on with it becoming quite the skill
Dare I let a lover touch upon my scaly arm
Watch again revulsion change a face that once held charm
Suffer more the comments and the questions all the same
'Why don't you put some cream on it', as if I was to blame
Like many things in life it must be treated from within
Although I ponder why so many see it as a sin
I ask myself what it is like to not feel constant pain
To have skin that is cool to touch as if I'm in the rain
I envy those whose skin is smooth and soft yet to the touch
It feels almost ridiculous to want something so much
Countless jokes at my expense begin to wear quite thin
Perhaps I should be grateful, for my ever thicker skin

PART 3

Rumination

Immortal Ruse

I realise with quite a fright
this page is now my portal
for as you read the words I write
I become immortal

who am I to deign to teach
ideas of my own
isn't this the overreach
what ideas I've sown

perhaps this is but idle thought
who could learn from me
I who give the gift of naught
can't tell you who to be

I can however here describe
present past not future
feelings I can here transcribe
pain that none can suture

always pain and never joy
tell me who would read
lamentations of a boy
broken hearts don't bleed

maybe I should turn the pen
over on its head
never once to mention men
ban all words of dread

every artist worth their salt
knows this is a lie
for pain is beauty by default
feeling others cry

cosy warm sunny light
nice and safe the day
picture now an endless night
praying for the grey

now see again through my soul
see a sorry hue
swirling into a deep hole
mingled black and blue

remember well my learned friend
to experience to bruise
believe survival till the end
drown in your own ruse

Who Am I

Tell me what you think of me
What is your first impression
You're looking at me nervously
I didn't want confession

So hard is it to say out loud
That which you think so true
You should in fact be very proud
Express what bothers you

See we all know just what I am
It's clear to all who gather
So let's not start a friendly sham
A dialogue of slather

Let's address the awful truth
I'm what you want to be
No longer just an ignorant youth
I've used my time you see

Through banal conversation hide
Hope and hidden fear
Extracted truths and hidden chide
A devil you keep near

And so you see with open eyes
I'm all that you created
Your best friend is to your surprise
Everything you hated

The Hue of You

I would I could create a hue
A hue encapsulating
You
The essence of this hue
I knew
Would be endearing through
(it's true)
And yet of all that knew
This hue
And did, as yet, not know
Of you
I wonder what to think
This hue
Would relate them back to
Not blue
But bold and live and strong
Right through
What colours might they then
Construe
If one has never felt
Of you
The way I feel when I
See you
And so I say I could
Pursue
A lifelong goal to find
The true
The colour breadth and depth
See through

Encapsulate the hue
Of you
Yet I wonder what they then
See too
For what if only I can view
This vibrant, True Hue of You?

Our Own Worst

I'll never fully understand, never comprehend
Why we seem unable to collectively send
A signal of our strength as a unified group
Instead we are caught in an undignified loop
Of continuous hurtful and deliberate betrayal
Plot each other's downfall and hope they she will fail
Who is she to come in here and tell me what to do
Why should I take orders from someone who is new
Never mind the background and experience at play
Never mind she tries to teach others every day
Surely, she has slept her way into such a position
We must ensure she undergoes quite the inquisition
Obvious, her efforts to teach those underneath
Stem from something sinister, soon she'll bare her teeth
Let's be sure we work against any calls for aid
Highlight to any we can if some mistake is made
Make it known quite clearly, she is on the out and out
Can't allow success stories to be getting about
Clearly she's a stepping stone for me to get above
She is in my way, so I had better give a shove
So caught in the competition that we fail to see
Given all the politics, roles now go to he
He that supports and values input from his peers
Amazing how such teamwork, leadership endears
Congratulations, yes, you've stopped her getting where she should
You've ensured that none of us will become what we could

Babysitter

Moving into town, we needed new arrangements
Someone had to help with children's entertainment
Babysit before, and for hours after school
And so, we met the family, they seemed really cool
A husband and a wife, with four of their own
They took in other children, hosted in their home
A couple of young boys, but both older than I
One of them was sullen, the other liked to cry
Their four children were split, two on each side
The boys made up the elders, the favourite hard to hide
And there my care was placed, into the family fair
And thus, began a life briefly full, of despair
It took a while to manifest, the torturous intent
Three of us were targets, for five of them to vent
For only when the father figure, home did return
Were we all safe, but this took a while to learn
He would make us toast, and ask about our day,
Only in his presence could the three of us play
When he wasn't present, away most of the week
Did she start her mind games, we became meek
One of us was chosen, one was singled out
Sometimes we didn't know what it was about
Only that we now had to suffer through the night
Once you were in trouble, you suffered quite a fright
Placed behind a lounge chair, watch her wheel it shut
Stuck here in the darkness, a little closed in hut
Seeing through a tiny crack as she brought out cake
Gives it to the others, proud was she to bake
Odd form of punishment for the child in care

Deliberately rewarding in front of one in there
This was how it started, slowly, building on
Strange to look back upon how she had the con
Worked into an art, telling each child not to tell
Your parents can't afford to leave, she knew we knew it well
Once they picked me up from school, in the big white van
The kids decided me today, they held down my hand
This is where the favourite, started then to pick
At the scab I had on it, until I felt quite sick
Pick and pick and pick again, until it came clean off
Bleeding on my little hand, bile turned into cough
I had never felt before such malicious action
For no better reason than, what, satisfaction?
Then being a little girl as I was of seven
How was I to know that telling this to her would threaten
Liar then she called and grabbed me by the hair
Pulled it over sink, hard, until my neck was bare
Confusion on my face as I only told the truth
My bleeding hand due to your rotten youth
Held me there until the pain made me say I lied
Let me go back to the couch where I sat and cried
Joined the other victims as we sat so very still
Not much left to do when you don't have free will
Her kids begin to kick a ball, the three of us we know
We are in big trouble when it goes through the window
None of us had moved, scared we were to breathe
Inside she did fly and at the three of us did seethe
I'll never forget when she pulled that leather belt
I don't know how no one picked up on such a welt
A welt we all bore quietly, reminded once again
Our parents were too poor to pay, so what then?

The daily fear of being dropped into such a den
Became a part of who I was, a burden, but then
Granny came to visit and took me home with her
Afternoons of joy and never fear would she incur
Then the time drew to a close, she asked me honestly
If I was happy to go back, expected words of glee
Expected me to miss my 'friends' and my routine
I shouted no before she finished, I knew then she'd seen
In my face the horror that was written, turned to lie
Said I didn't mean that, I just didn't want goodbye
Granny always knew me best and so she teased it out
All the fear melted away, all the lies and doubt
Family were mortified, at least I saved the others
None of us were brave enough, none of us had brothers
Only children were we three, lonely but together
If we could stand that hellish den, we'll be strong forever
Babysitter moved away to escape the shame
Sitting in another state, she deserves the fame
Instead she gets to slink away and never mind disgrace
I hope to god I never see her rounded friendly face

Mettle and Flesh

I don't remember why or what
what made me run so fast, but
downstairs my legs did fly and I
I watched them hurtle past.
I never gave much thought, to
to how much noise I made, and
being quite distraught, you
yelled at me, forbade, the
unrelenting screaming, I
directed at you both, because
once again we moved and
this place was really gross, with
roaches in the walls and
we had left the beach and
yet another school where
no more friends in reach, but
back to where we are, you
caught me by the arm
to be honest I never thought
you could do me harm, so
when you grabbed my hair, you
lifted tiny form, only nine
I wasn't tall, into the air,
thin and small, drag up stairs
staccato pops as my shins
hit every stop. What a din
I remember every bone
hitting pop, I'm not stone
lucky that I didn't crack

grateful not pulled on my back
did you then need to whack
back hand across my face
as you pulled me in the door
to be honest I remember
not crying any more, as
you really wouldn't stop
I entered into shock
she screamed at you to stop
then she left, too much to bear
as you stood there with my hair, and
stormed out with disgrace,
as if she had injured face, but then
memory of sitting, of a mirror
of a vision, a horror, looking back,
cheeks so swollen couldn't hide, that
something had just died, the
young girl looking back had
inside her newest crack not
a crack but a chasm, once
an adult, cannot fathom, how
you pushed my flesh to metal
just a child, little petal, what
lessons you impart, when
you bruise children's hearts.

Thoughts & Prayers

Is it really fair
the way we let it go
We never say a word but we know,
we all know
We watch it from afar,
and do not raise a hand
We turn our heads away,
we cannot watch,
cannot stand
Who are we to judge
and dare we interfere
It doesn't happen often never here,
never here
We are but a few,
what were we to do
How were we to know it would be you,
next you
Then we get the grief,
we get to feel forlorn
We cluster altogether as we mourn,
we do mourn
We whisper in the corners,
we say it isn't right
We mention it in forums,
but rarely will we fight
We settle back to patterns
and comfort in the norm
We want to see it go away,
another passing storm

And yet the clouds they gather
And so it comes again
Ready all your thoughts and prayers
Let the bullets reign

Asleep

I wake
And I look up
The spiral staircase is full
Every one of us has a step
And so we take it
Ever marching
Where?
I shudder
I look down
At the rows of us behind
All dutifully stepping towards me
I lean to see how many
God, how many
And then I fall
Past the husks
Shuffling
For so long
And yet no end in sight
Before I am caught by him
By the only one who sees
His eyes not sewn shut
But fully open, like me
He swings me
Onto the step behind
He takes another step forward
He looks me dead in the eye
'Don't fall again'
I fear
I wake

Writer's Compulsion

I see you as you write yourself
pouring from my mind
alarming yet I find

The words cascade from hand to page
from finger into font
it's not something I want

Not something which I can control
the clacking of the keys
all other thoughts they freeze

Until the idea is put forth
to stop it spinning around
bring me back to ground

Compulsion is so hard to stop
physical the need
like an internal bleed

Giving in feels like release
the leaking thoughts to launch
in order pain to staunch

Cathartic as process may be
it's hard to understand
why can't I stay my hand?